MW01701475

The Art of

This is a work of art brought about by vision, creativity, imagination, and curiosity. A product produced and delivered by the author. Any compounded interpretations of this product are entirely unique to the reader.

The Conversion
Book design by Gary Hensche Cover design by Gary Hensche
ISBN: 9798991240284

Published by Gary Hensche

Follow me on media

Dedication

I would like to begin by dedicating The Art of to history; an era in which my curiosity and my mind first dove into something far out of my realm. A dedication to the memories behind an era, the fall.

Where to begin? My heart is all over the board. It's done been broken, shattered, scattered, taped, glued, filled, then stepped on, scraped up, tossed away, and an endless array of other things, and at this point, I'm curious about when the love begins. From me to you, the love begins now. For that, I dedicate The Conversion.

I would like to dedicate The Art of to the Chinese culture. I hope with The Conversion, I can earn, build, and then maintain the respect of the Chinese culture. By no means do I mean anything of The Art of other than to respect the teachings of ancient Chinese culture in ways that they have not been fully respected. For that, I dedicate The Art of.

I would like to dedicate The Art of to all the businessmen and business women. Whether you like a short read, an interesting read, or an insightful read. To you I dedicate The Conversion.

I would like to dedicate The Art of to all the military men and woman. Whether you realize it or not you are more than a warrior. In the darkest of days may The Art of remind you that you belong to this world and to keep your chin up. To you I dedicate The Art of.

I would like to dedicate The Conversion to you, the reader. I thank you for your support and hope to continuously earn this support by bringing you material that doesn't just fulfill your life but the lives of our children for years to come. To you, I dedicate The Art of.

Finally, I would like to dedicate The Art of to the organizations and platforms that embrace the The Conversion. Without you, this wouldn't be possible.

I would also like to take the time to dedicate The Art of to a new beginning.

Acknowledgment

I would like to acknowledge the hidden truth of the era in which my curiosity and mind first dove into something far out of my realm. Many things happened since then and my life and the lives of my family will never be the same.

I would like to acknowledge the era of great warlords and leaders such as Alexander the Great, Leonidas, Genghis Khan, and, of course, Sun Tzu; know that these four leaders do not stand alone. These are all individuals who earned the respect of so many people with their endless depth of great heroic, fearless, and fearful leadership. What about Maximus Decimus Meridius of Rome? Are great leaders like these and the Joan of Arc a myth? Did Robin Hood not exist?

I would like to acknowledge that leaders as such may be much more than just about war and the bloodshed war brings about; soon, you will be acknowledging this too.

I acknowledge The Conversion as a means of help versus bloodshed, and I acknowledge that is where I want you by the end of this book. As tough as it sounds, acknowledge the good this book can do for you and countless individuals you don't even know.

I would like to acknowledge The Art of as a light, your light. A light that millions of people have never imagined, let alone seen. May this light shine on dark spots in your life and help redirect you toward an amazing life you have only imagined. I acknowledge that The Conversion is for you.

I would like to acknowledge you, readers. I bet many of you has read more than I have in a lifetime. My son, too, has probably surpassed that by now. As I attempt to prove that you don't necessarily have to be the biggest reader to write a book, I acknowledge that you must be a reader to read a book, and on that note, I thank you. I thank you for being a reader.

I acknowledge that even though you readers have done more than I could ask by reading The Conversion, I ask of you that you use whatever you pull from it for good towards you and all others you are blessed to encounter throughout your lives. I ask you to understand that you never just harm one person. Be a light and, if possible, not their darkness.

Finally, I would like to acknowledge the series The Art of and its books beginning with The Conversion.

I would like to acknowledge all the difficulties with The Conversion. I hope that it touches all of your hearts and mind.

I acknowledge the hope of a new beginning for you, an era which enriches your life and the lives of many others.

I want to acknowledge The Art of as your light.

This is Real

Disclosure Statement

Throughout this book, you will see how a book written centries ago before the birth of Christ can be translated into modern business. Keep in mind when reading the book that it revolves around war. As the great Sun Tzu states, "Only one who is thoroughly acquainted with the evils of war can thoroughly understand the profitable way of carrying it on." Keep in mind that in war, on the extreme side, people die. Through the act of war, individuals are hurt, loved ones are hurt, and lives can be forever damaged. So, it is said to you that how you decide to go about your daily life and utilize the information you collect from the series The Art of is your sole decision.

The author, Gary Hensche, of The Art of The Conversion is not responsible for any acts and behavior from anyone who heeds the words written in The Art of The Conversion. The author of The Art of The Conversion,Gary Hensche, is not responsible for the consequences someone might suffer from the acts someone might choose in response to the information obtained while reading The Art of The Conversion. The author Gary Hensche doesn't guarantee the information in The Art of The Conversion to be the most dominant information in the field nor guarantees The Art of The Conversion to be the solution to any of your problems. The author Gary Hensche isn't responsible for how the manipulated words brought about from The Art of The Conversion is used. Know that people suffer daily because of decisions, and if that decision is to exist, then it is your responsibility to own it and nobody else's.

The Art of The Conversion is designed to take the text of a respected book written many years ago and expose it in a new light. Again, it is not the author Gary Hensche's responsibility for how this information is understood and/or used. It isn't the author Gary

Hensche's responsibility for any actions taken before or after reading The Art of The Conversion. It isn't the author Gary Hensche's responsibility for any consequences, good or bad, that someone might experience because of The Art of The Conversion and/or any of the information in the book The Art of The Conversion, which was not used in good heart or any manner of heart for that fact.

So once more, I say to you that your actions to read any books belonging to the series The Art of including The Conversion was your decision. Any knowledge you embrace while and after reading the series The Art of including The Conversion is yours to use at your discretion, which you are responsible for.

There is a version of the Art of War by James Clavell that I believe rings some truth. James Clavell stated, "I believe very much that Sun Tzu's knowledge is vital to our survival. It can give us the protection we need to watch our children grow in peace and thrive. Always remember since ancient times, it has been known that the true object of war is peace."

The Conversion

一 (Yī) Planning 1

1. Business, like war, is essential for a nation's prosperity. Success hinges on Planning. Leadership in business, paralleling the general's role, acts as a bulwark, crucial for both organisation triumph and the broader economic well-being, linking the state's prosperity to global dynamics.

2. Business is a matter of life and death, a path either to prosperity or to poverty for both organisation and economic well-being. Therefore, it is a topic that must not be overlooked.

3. Organisations are guided by five factors that must be considered.

4. The Five Foundational Factors are:

   (1) Corporate Culture & Ethics: Moral Law
   (2) Market Dynamics & Trends: Heaven
   (3) Operational Assets & Capabilities: Earth
   (4) Organization Vision & Decisiveness: The Commander
   (5) Strategic & Procedural Discipline: Method and Discipline

5. ;6. Culture & Ethics: Moral Law

   The first factor, culture & ethics, is a moral understanding that steers employee behavior. The principles, proclaimed values, and ethical limits mold the way decisions being made impact one another. Culture often shapes around both company and employee which leads to a commitment from all parties and is often viewed externally.

7. Product & Trends: Heaven

   The second factor, products and trends, embraces awareness of both the internal and external operating environment. Products and Trends fall victim to supply and demand cycles which determines the growth or decline of the organisation. Shifting consumer preferences lead to product innovation or obsolescence. The market includes economic indicators like consumer sentiment trajectories, buyer demographic shifts, technology disruptions, supply chain developments, competitive innovations, adjacent sector convergence, and more.

8. Assets & Asset Capabilities: Earth

   Assets and asset capabilities is a driving force behind progress. Assets and asset capabilities are often determined by things like scaling, strategic positions, risk management, and opportunities for future success. The operational capacities of assets shape and often limits the realm of possibility. Assets and capabilities are in connection across core operations—including but not limited to production, technology systems, distribution channels, supply chain and its relationships, research and development, and real estate. The capability of an asset is the driving force of a vision.

9. Vision & Capability: The Commander

   The fourth factor, provided by vision and capability, requires an understanding of the vision. The vision itself brings capabilities in which brings an organisation into a realm of opportunities. A true understanding of characteristics brings more understanding to capabilities, ultimately enhancing the ability of a vision. Strategic coherence, signaling, commitment, trust, and understanding are all great qualities and capabilities. Planning, order, timing, delivery, and execution is important for understanding. Capabilities, decisiveness compassion, integrity, self-discipline, intelligence, and authenticity deliver a vision.

10. Strategic & Procedural Discipline: Method and Discipline
    Strategic & Procedural Discipline in Business involves:

    (1) Strict communication of all roles, organisational structure, policy, and tasks; communication for everything which then sets the boundaries for discipline.

(2) Implementing clear hierarchical structures for order and career advancement.
(3) Ensuring operational route for resource flow and expansion.
(4) Managing resources within boundaries of communication, law, and order.
(5) The written methods or best practices which hold constant to delivering efficiently and effectively in terms of execution.

11. These five factors should be well-understood by every organisation: Those who master them will succeed; those who neglect them will face setbacks.

12. When an organisation is planning let it assess competitive business conditions, consider these five factors for and in comparison.

13. Organisations shall contemplate these seven considerations when planning:
(1) Which of the two organizations demonstrates stronger moral law, ethical values, and corporate culture?
(2) Which of the organisations exhibit greater abilities?
(3) Which organisation has the advantage in heaven and earth, market conditions, and operational capabilities?
(4) Which organisation is most disciplined to method and discipline?
(5) Which organisation has greater resources, whether in terms of financial strength, human capital, or technological assets?
(6) Which organisation is stronger, better trained, and more skilled?
(7) In which organisation is there more consistency to rewards and punishments?

14. Through these seven considerations, progress or setbacks can be determined.

15. Organisations that can fully understand The Art of "The Conversion" may be successful. An organisation that does not may face failure.

16. While leveraging the benefits of planned guidance an organization should also seize opportunities that arise beyond the standard practices.

17. Plans shall be modified when situations favor and adjust the organisation's business plans toward long-term objectives as short-term goals are reached.

18. Organisation planning involves an element of deception.

19. Hence, when an organisation can go on the offensive, it must appear not to be; when actively pursuing opportunities, it must appear not to be; when close to opportunity, it must make competition believe it's far away; when objections are far away, it must make competition believe it's close.

20. Organisational movement presents opportunity on both sides; questionable movement insinuates uncertainty. Capitalize on the competitions miscalculations.

21. If competition is well-established, plan accordingly. If competition holds a dominant stance, avoid confrontation.

22. If your competition is of haste temper, seek to exploit it. Conceal some ability to encourage self-importance.

23. If competition is acting with simplicity, an organisation must keep them engaged. If they act with unity, an organisation must seek to disrupt them.

24. Compete where competition is least prepared, orchestrate in a manner not expected.

25. These organisational devices and information, leading to success, should not be revealed in advance.

26. Organisations that succeed make many calculations prior to. Organisations that fail make few calculations. If many calculations lead to success and few calculations to failure: What are the consequences of no calculation? Understanding this, organisations can forecast likeliness of success or the likeliness of failure.

二 (Èr) The Field 2

1. It is said: In organisational functions, where there are quantities of assets, potentially thousands of employees and third-party individuals, and mass quantities of resources to carry the organisation, the expense of both latent and in progress, including benefits, rewards, and milestone celebrations, will reach the total of a large non-fixed cost per day. Such is the cost to train and maintain an organization of any size.

2. When an organisation is on the offense, the progress is long-term, assets will depreciate, the organisations morale and character will be affected. When an organisation pursues progress, it will exhaust its strength.

3. If organisational campaigns are prolonged, the resources of the sovereign will not equal the expense.

4. Now, when an organisations assets are depreciated, the team's morale and character are low, organisation reserves are spent, competition will seize opportunities. No organisation, no matter its abilities, will be able to prevent the consequences.

5. Thus, organisations have heard of carelessness in operations and that intelligence has never been associated with procrastination.

6. There is no instance of an organisation having benefited from lengthy direct or indirect offensive conflict.

7. It is only the organisation thoroughly acquainted with the downfalls of business that can thoroughly understand the profitable way of conducting it.

8. An organisation avoids gathering and distributing excess resources, nor are the organisation's supply chains loaded more than twice.

9. Distribute resources from the organisation but forage from the local community. Thus, the organisation will have what it needs.

10. Poverty of the organisation's sovereign causes the organisation to maintain from the use of external funding. Contributing to maintaining an organisation at a distance like so causes the organisation to become impoverished.

11. On the other hand, the proximity of an organisation causes prices to rise, and high prices cause the organisations substance to be drained.

12. When an organisations substance is drained, the peasantry of the organisation and the local community will be affected.

13. ;14. With the loss of organisation and peasantry substance and exhaustion of strength, both organisation and peasantry homes will suffer consequences, investments and income will then begin to dissipate, while the Sovereigns expenses for asset depreciation consume a vast portion of an organisation's total revenue.

15. Hence, an organisation will forage off the competition and local community. A cartload of theirs is to twenty of the organisations.

16. To encourage and inflict morale, the organisation must be motivated and focused. There may be a purpose behind the cause, they must have benefits, their rewards.

17. To maximize organisational gains, when significant achievements are reached, those who achieved them first and greatest should be rewarded in the way they achieved, first and greatest. All contributors should be acknowledged. The organisation shall inherit any assets and resources and use them in conjunction with its own. Any individuals suffering from the evils of war should be treated kindly and, with their approval, kept as an asset and utilized for their skills.

18. This is called leveraging competition's gains for organisational use.

19. In business, then, let organisational objectives be success, not various lengthy campaigns.

20. Thus, it may be known that leaders of an organisation are the authority of the peoples fate, the entities on whom decides whether the people of the nation will be at peace or peril.

三 (Sān) Stratagem 3

1. In business, the best thing of all is to acquire the competition as a whole and intact; to shatter the competition and destroy them is not so good. So too, it is better to recapture the competition entirely than to destroy them, to recapture a location, a district, a region, or the organisation entirely than to destroy it.

2. Hence, to achieve success and be victorious in every objective is not the highest form of excellence; the highest form of excellence is to overcome objectives without fighting.

3. Thus, the highest form of an organisation is to balk the competition's plans; the next best is to prevent the junction of the competition's forces. The next in order is to offensively compete with the competition in the field; and the worst policy of all is to offensively compete with the competition strictly adhering to direct methods alone.

4. The rule is to not directly engage in prolonged conflict if it can be avoided. The preparation of organization assets, inventory, and resources takes a considerable amount of time; further efforts require even more time.

5. The organisation, controlled by frustration, will fail to plan accordingly, with the result that a considerable portion of labor will be misused and success will still not be obtained. Such are the disastrous effects of a project.

6. Therefore, a skillful organization overcomes without difficulty; they capture success without fully engaging; they overcome without lengthy operations in the field.

7. With the organisation intact, it will dispute competition, without fatal resistance, the organisation will triumph. This method is known as attacking by stratagem.

8. It is a rule in business if organisation forces are most to few, to surround the competition; if more to few, to attack the competition; if twice as much to the competition, to divide the forces equally.

9. If an organisation is equally matched, it may invite competition; If they are slightly inferior, they may avoid the competition; if they are unequal in every way, they may flee from the competition.

10. Hence, although a smaller organisation may compete rather well, in the end, it must be contained by the larger force.

11. Now, leaders of an organisation are like the bulwark of the State; if the bulwark is complete at all points; the State will be strong; if the bulwark is defective, the state will be weak.

12. There are three ways in which an organisation can bring misfortune upon its people:

13. (1) By commanding the organisation to advance or retreat, being ignorant of the fact that it cannot obey. This is called hobbling the organisation.

14. (2) By attempting to govern an organisation in the way in which a nation would be governed and being ignorant of the conditions obtained in an army. This causes restlessness in the soldier's mind.

15. (3) By employing the leaders of an organization without discrimination through ignorance of the organisational principle of adaptation to circumstances. This may shake the confidence of the people.

16. When restless and distrustful, trouble is sure to come from competition. This simply brings rebellion into the organisation and flings success away.

17. Thus, we may know there are five essentials for success:
   (1) To knows when to compete and when not to compete.
   (2) To knows how to handle both superior and inferior forces.
   (3) Whose followers are animated by the same spirit throughout all its ranks.
   (4) That prepares themselves and waits to take the competition unprepared.
   (5) That has the competitive capacity and is not interfered with by the sovereign.

18. If you understand both the organisation and its competition, you will be able to navigate numerous business challenges successfully. If you understand the organisation but not the competition, for every success, you may also face setbacks. If you lack the understanding of both the organisation and the competition, there will be difficulties in all business endeavors.

四 (Sì) Tactics I 4

1. Organisations put themselves beyond the possibilities of failure and then look for opportunities given by their competition.

2. For an organisation to secure itself from defeat lies in its own ability, but the opportunity to defeat is provided by the competition.

3. Good organisations can secure themselves against defeat but cannot make certain of defeating the competitor. Strong organisations can secure themselves from failure but cannot directly overcome competitors.

4. Therefore, it's acknowledged that an organisation may know how to outperform without having the means or care to.

5. An organisations stability involves defensive tactics; the capability to outperform involves initiating offensive actions.

6. Maintaining a defensive stance signals a lack of strength; but taking an offensive position signals an abundance of strength.

7. Organisations that excel in defense operate offensively with subtlety and caution accepting security over risk, akin to being hidden, whereas organisations skilled in offense emerges efficiently and effectively with the heavens. Thus, on one side, the capability to safeguard, and on the other, the potential for expansion.

8. Recognizing opportunity when obvious does not represent the highest level of tactical capability.

9. It is not the essence of organisational achievement to succeed and the whole organisation to applaud.

10. Achieving easy is no indication of significant capability; to see what is already expected as the norm does not signify

exceptional insight; to hear directly is no sign of a quick ear.

11. To be remembered as a tactical strategist is to achieve efficiently and effectively.

12. Therefore, achievements do not earn an organisation widespread acclaim for being wise or brave.

13. Organisations gain the most by avoiding errors. Avoiding errors ensure the likelihood of success, for it means overcoming challenges that have already been mitigated.

14. Thus, the adept organisation positions in a way that failure is impossible and does not wait to seize an opportunity.

15. In business, the successful strategist only engages offensively after success is already achieved, whereas organisations destined for offense enter and then seek ways to succeed.

16. The masterful organisation fosters moral law and swiftly adopts systematic approaches to method and discipline; thereby, it is the organisations ability to influence success.

17. Regarding the organisation in business tactics, firstly, assessment; secondly, estimation of resource; thirdly, calculation; fourthly, risk evaluation; and fifthly, success.

18. Assessment is grounded in the market environment; estimation of resources is to assessment; calculation stems from estimation of resources; risk evaluation is from calculation; and success is from risk evaluation.

19. A successful organisation, as opposed to a failing one, is the advantage in resources and tactics compared to another.

20. The surge of a successful organisation is like the release of energies and resources into deep markets, which is the essence of tactics in business.

五 (Wǔ) Energy 5

1. Managing a large team is the same as managing a small team: it is a matter of how you divide the numbers.

2. Working with a large organisation under your guidance is no different than with a small one: it is just a matter of clear communication.

3. To ensure that your organisation can withstand the worst of competition and remain competitive- this is achieved by stratagem both direct and indirect.

4. That the impact of your organisation be of such effect as if leadership had known the knowledge behind weak points and strong points.

5. In all businesses, the direct strategy may be used to engage competition, but indirect methods is to achieve an organisations success.

6. Indirect tactics, efficiently executed, are inexhaustible as heaven and earth, much like the fluency of the four seasons, one season ends to begin a new one and only to cycle through all to return once more.

7. There may be limited business principles, yet in combination, these principles give rise to more strategem than a scenario needs.

8. There may be limited primary strategies, yet in combination, they give rise to more strategem than a scenario needs.

9. There may be limited tactics, yet in combination, these tactics give rise to more stratagem than a scenario needs.

10. In business, there are not more than two offensive methods, direct and indirect; yet these two, in combination, give rise to more stratagem than a scenario needs.

11. The direct and the indirect business methods lead to each other in turn. This interplay is cyclical and continuous. Who can exhaust their unending possibilities?

12. The launch of business initiatives is silent, quick, engaged, well planned, and well executed, capable of moving obstacles and achieving success.

13. The quality of decision are akin to the precision and timing of execution, crucial for ensuring strategic moves and successful outcomes.

14. Therefore, an organisation may not be so structured in the beginning but prompt in its decisions.

15. An organisation's energy is compared to the preparation of its decision to the releasing of the momentum.

16. In the midst of competing, there may be a sense of disorder yet none at all; amidst this illusion, an organisation may appear flat but still capable of success.

17. What appears to be disorder to one may actually be the display of perfect discipline from another. An organisation hesitant to advance might suggest a lack of confidence; an organisation in which weakness is obvious may just be representation.

18. Organisations concealing stratagem under disorganization involves subdivisions; concealing ability behind timidity may suggest a reserve of unused energy; cloaking an organisations strength with weakness may be influenced by tactical dispositions.

19. An organisation skilled at keeping the competition on the move maintains questionable positions offering thought for the competition to respond. To sacrifice so that the competition might move.

20. By presenting opportunity, the competition stays engaged. While being observant and prepared, the organisation may plan accordingly.

21. The organisation structures to the use of combined energy, not expecting too much from individuals. Hence, the ability to employ accordingly and maximize the use of combined energy.

22. When using compounded energy, the organisation progresses. The nature of the organisation is to remain operational, but with energies combined, they begin to progress. Operatable organisations remain still, but by utilizing combined energy, they expand.

23. Thus, the energy generated is like momentum compounded through success. So much about energy that is compounded and harnessed from business success.

六 (Liù) S.W.O.T. 6

1. The organisation to first enter a market puts itself at an advantage, ready and prepared; second, in a market, possibly rushed will arrive more exhausted of strength.

2. Therefore, the knowledgeable organisation imposes the competition, but does not allow the competition's will to be imposed on it.

3. By holding out potential benefits to the competition, the organisation can cause them to approach on its own accord, or, by inflicting damage, the organisation can make it impossible for them to draw near.

4. If the organisation is taking its ease, competition can harass them; if well supplied with resources, competition can starve the organisation out; if quietly encamped, the competition can force the organisation to move or make a move.

5. Appear at points which the competition must hasten to defend; move the organisation into spaces where it is not expected.

6. An organisation may progress great distances without distress if on markets the competition is not.

7. The organisation can only be sure of succeeding in its direct methods if the organisation competes upon areas undefended by competition. The organisation can ensure the safety of its defenses if it only holds positions that cannot be competed with.

8. Hence, an organisation is skillful in attack whose competition does not know what to defend, and an organisation is skillful in defense whose competition does not know what to attack.

9. Elusive and Stealth! Through these words, an organisation learns to be invisible. Through these words, it learns to be inaudible, and hence, an organisation can hold the competition's fate in its hands.

10. An organisation may progress and be irresistible if it makes for the competitor's weak points; the organisation may divert and regroup from competition if it's movements are more rapid.

11. If an organisation wishes to engage directly, its competition can be forced to engage even though it can be sheltered behind some form of defense. All the organisation needs to do is directly pursue another place that the competition will be obliged to relieve.

12. If an organisation doesn't choose to engage directly, it can prevent the competition from engaging even though lines in the organisation's position can be traced out on the ground.

13. By discovering the competition's disposition and by the organisation remaining elusive, the organisation can keep its forces concentrated while the competition's must be divided.

14. An organisation can form as a single unit, while the competition must divide into fractions. Hence, a single unit pitted against parts of a unit, which means an organisation may be many to the competition's few.

15. If an organisation is capable of competing with an inferior force with a superior force, the competition will be in a serious position.

16. The position an organisation intends to take must not be known, for the competition will have to prepare against possible advancements to several different points, and the competition thus distributes and deploys in many directions, the numbers an organization will have to face at any given point will be fewer.

17. Should the competition strengthen their advance guard, the competition will weaken his tail; should the competition strengthen his tail, the competition will weaken his advance

guard; should the competition strengthen his left, the competition will weaken his right; should the competition strengthens his right, the competition will weaken his left. If the competition sends reinforcements everywhere, the competition will be weak everywhere.

18. Numerical weakness to an organization comes from having to prepare against advancements from competition; numerical strength to an organisation from compelling our competitors to make these preparations against us.

19. For an organisation to know the place and time of a coming conflict, it may concentrate from the greatest distances to fight.

20. But if neither time nor place is known to an organisation, then the left wing will be less effective helping the right, the right equally less effective helping the left, and the advance guard unable to relieve the rear.

21. Though, according to the estimate, a competitors strengths may exceed an organisation's strengths, that shall be to the advantage of the competition, but not to the matter of victory. Progress can be achieved.

22. Though the competition be stronger in numbers, an organisation may prevent direct methods against it. Work to discover the competition's plans and the likelihood of its success.

23. Understand the competition and learn the reasoning of their activity or inactivity. Assist the competitor in revealing themselves and find out their vulnerable spots.

24. Compare the competitor to the organisation so that you may know where strength is and know where strength is not.

25. When determining tactics the quality of mind is the highest tier an organisation can attain to reveal such strength; conceal dispositions, and the organisation will be free from the probing of spies.

26. How success may come for the organisation from the competition's own tactics- that is what the masses cannot comprehend.

27. All can see the tactics whereby an organisation succeeds, but what nobody can see is the strategy in which success evolved.

28. Do not repeat tactics that earned an organisation a single success, but let methods be controlled by the endless variety of circumstances.

29. Business tactics fluid; naturally fluids flows away from high places and hastens downwards.

30. So, in business, avoid strong points and strike at what is weak points.

31. An organisation should shape its strategy as circumstances demand, like fluid over the course it flows.

32. Thus, just as fluids changes form, an organisation favors no constant conditions in business.

33. The organisation that can modify tactics in relation to competition and thereby achieves success may be called a heaven-born organisation.

34. Factors of heaven aren't all equally predominant. Seasons change and natural signs and signals change with the seasons.

七 (Qī) Movement 7

1. In business, the organisation receives its commands from the market, shareholder, stakeholder, customer demands, or the sovereign.

2. After the organisation has assembled its assets and concentrated its forces, the organisation must calculate its position before determining its location.

3. Following is tactical maneuvering which is never so easy. To turn devious into direct and unfortunate situations into gain is never easy with tactical maneuvering.

4. For an organisation to take an indirect route after luring the competition out of the way, to strive to achieve the same goal before the competitor, shows the cleverness of deviation.

5. Maneuvering a business is advantageous, without method and discipline most dangerous.

6. An organisation that fully prepares to grasp an advantage will likely be too late. These advantages may mean being less prepared.

7. Over-exhausting resources and people risks falling.

8. The strongest members will maintain the lead while the others shall follow, meaning around one-tenth of it's driven staff will reach such a destination.

9. A less exhausted crew attempting to capture a sudden opportunity will lose its first leader, and half the organisation's force will reach their objectives.

10. An organisation with an even less exhausted team will lose its first leader to capture sudden opportunity with a result of approximately two-thirds of it's force reaching its objectives.

11. An unprepared workforce, underequipped and exhausted, is considered lost.

12. An organisation cannot enter an alliance without first knowing the structure of the party with which it may be ally with.

13. An organisation is not fit to lead its army unless it's aware of the earth in which it intends to cross.

14. To make full use of its natural abilities and to fulfill its purpose an organisation must make use of local signals and information.

15. In business, an organisation may move to deceive, but without a cause, there is no need to move.

16. To either consolidate or separate assets must be done by situation.

17. An organisation's offensive movement shall be quick, and when it's defensive it will expand less, and consolidate.

18. Movement should only be to consume what is in a path. The organisation should be in scope and undeterred by distractions.

19. An organisation shall keep its plans hidden and protected When it moves it should strike quickly.

20. When an organisation feeds off the local community, divide the assets amongst the itself. When the organisation expands, let the use be for employment.

21. An organisation should give deep thought and many calculations before it moves.

22. An organisation will progress further the more it understands the value in what is visibly gained from its efforts versus the gains that were expected to prevent unexpected losses. Such is the grace in movement.

23. As seen in business, the voice doesn't carry the distance needed. Hence the need for interfaces, databases, signs and signals. Nor may organisation objectives and guiding be

clear: so, let there be legislation, SOPs, notes, and reminders.

24. When using effective communication an organization can keep the teams in scope and on point.

25. Creating a single force where no individual succeeds or fails alone.

26. Organisations exploring blind grounds, let some movements be seen and make use of research, data, and competitor insights. When on familiar ground convert to company information and communication.

27. In business morale may be lost, and the organisation may fall uncertain.

28. A man's ability is sharpest in the morning, but by mid-day, not so. By evening, he is ready to call it a day.

29. An organisation knows to avoid competitors when there at their sharpest. Advance mid-day or in the later when comfort sets in. This is a thought behind the stages of business.

30. Organisations should remain at its peak and be patient as it waits for opportunity exposed by its competitors.

31. Being closer to the objective than the competitor, to wait while they may struggle, to provide while they are not: - preserving strength.

32. Avoid engaging a competitor who is in perfect form. Avoid competing with competitors who are cool and collected:- study the circumstances.

33. An organisation should avoid uphill battles. No need to interfere as the competition is moving downhill.

34. Do not pursue withdrawing competition . Nor should they be pursued when they are at their sharpest.

35. Stay on plan, in scope, and concentrated, fall for no bait or lures presented by competition. Don't interfere with them when they are pulling back.

36. An organisation shouldn't fully surround the competitor but leave an outlet instead. Do not puss them too hard.

八 (Bā) Tactics II 8

1. In business, the organisation gives the command, it gathers its army and consolidates its forces.

2. An organisation that is not firmly grounded should remain offensive until secure. When its goals are not timely, they should reach out. Do not become relaxed in a position that is not secured. When in a difficult position be sure to use strategy. In a dire situation put up a fight.

3. There are roads that must not be followed. There is competition that should not be directly assaulted. There will be competition that is best to leave alone.

4. An organisation that knows the purpose of various tactics will know how to train, disperse, and best use its troops.

5. An organisation that doesn't understand the use of various tactics may know heaven and earth but still not be able to turn knowledge into progress.

6. The leader still young in the Art of War and the varying of plans, even knowing the factors and conditions to business will fail to utilize its men best.

7. Intelligent plans have the understanding of different scenarios, cause and effect, positives and negatives, hindsight and foresight, profits and losses. All calculations will come together in a single plan.

8. If an organisation expects to progress, it is hardened through planning, and they may succeed in the essential part of its plans.

9. In the toughest of times, an organisation is ready to progress through an opportunity. At this point, the organisation may relieve itself of difficulties.

10. Meanwhile, during the toughest of times, if an organisation is ready to progress through opportunity, it may relieve itself from the difficulty that has not yet presented itself.

11. An organisation recognizes that it is best to prepare itself against competition and the ability to progress. It knows not to ready itself on the assumption that competition will not progress on them but instead make their defenses unbreakable.

12. There are five faults to an organisation.
    (1) Carelessness: Conducting business without considering plans and calculations. Diverting of plans can lead to strategic mistakes.
    (2) Procrastination: A fear of taking risks leads to loss opportunities. To assume theres tomorrow leads to failure.
    (3) Wrong Attitude: A fault that leads to assumption, miscalculation, bad charisma, and can cause an organisation to react impulsively.
    (4) Emotions: Being over burdened by emotions one way or the other leads to bad decision. If bad decision can come on emotions what truth comes from fact and data. What is best for what's at stake.
    (5) Excessive Concern: for employee leads to emotions and other troubles. For the work performed shows a lack of trust and confidence.

13. These five faults are negatives to an organisation and the conduct of business.

14. When an organisation fails its leaders do too and these faults are amongst these faults. An organisation should take the time to consider such a subject.

九 (Jiǔ) Operations 9

1. An organisation will need to decide on location and where it will be located needs to be determined in secrecy. Expansion should be done quickly. Placing a careful eye on competition and to pass over to where they elevate themselves may aid in these decisions .

2. Position yourself on precipitous heights facing the light of truth. Never climb heights just to compete.

3. An organisation that crosses rough terrain knows it is best to stray away from like situation.

4. It is best to advance on competition amidst its struggles. There is no need to meet the competitor in the middle of such circumstances.

5. If an organisation is eager to compete, it is best not to meet them at the border of rough terrain.

6. An organisation of high efficiency should instill it through the ranks and subdivisions in light of truth. Do not engage a competitor in an upstream manner So much for fluid motion, efficiency and effectiveness.

7. With concerns about difficult grounds and terrain, it is best for an organisation to get over them quickly.

8. If forced to compete on difficult grounds remain closest to financial and product resources with safety at your rear, where the organisation is most dense. So much for operating on difficult grounds.

9. On less lucrative grounds you should have room to rise on one flank and your rear. Competition is always forward and behind lies the safety of the organisation, where it is most dense.

10. An organisation that acknowledges these four tiers of competition knowledge finds that they enable it to overcome four tiers and several sovereigns.

11. Prefer secure positions over not and the light of truth over uncertainty.

12. If an organisation is careful in its delegating and remains firm on the grounds of method and discipline, it will be free of difficulty, and success will follow.

13. When it comes to a rise then you should choose the uphill side of difficulty and truth. Leave the slope at your rear. Thus you will be acting right for your people and leading the organisation towards the natural advantage given by grounds of progress.

14. When circumstances forbid success, you should know prior to competing and that it is best to wait.

15. When both heaven and earth bring too much difficulty in achieving progress then such grounds should be avoided. The organisation should leave these grounds as quickly as possible.

16. While staying clear of unfavored grounds try to create or direct the competition to such grounds. While facing the competitor they may have the difficult grounds and position of uncertainty at their rear.

17. On uncertain and difficult ground heaven and earth should diligently be considered. For these are the most difficult to navigate and provide much uncertainty. There may lie hidden opportunity and risks. Advantages may exist for both you and your competitor if ill-prepared.

18. When latent and not visually expanding an organisation is relying on its current position and strengths.

19. When an organisation fears not the consequences of vision, it is anxious for the competitor to proceed.

20. Organisation's offering room to advance, is offering bait and inviting competition.

21. Expansion or new competitors sharing the same grounds and market is a sign to embrace for the new competition. The visuals of preparation brings forth uncertainty.

22. Hearing voices, competitor movement, and market shifts are all signs leading back to competition movement. Direct competitors shaken by movements is a direct threat.

23. When an organisation is most concentrated on a terrain, the supply will be most concentrated and advancement will be quick. When concentration is spread out, so is the supply and advancement will be slower. When the signs of advancement are broad they are in the stages of planning. As the signs settle it signifies determination.

24. An organisation that speaks appropriately and adequately prepares; these are warning signs of possible advancement. When it becomes more hostile and pushes forward, these are signs of a possible retreat.

25. When the first of supply reaches the flanks, it is a sign that the competitor is to compete.

26. A proposal toward any agreement without a written agreement amongst the parties involved indicates a plot.

27. Supply and demand being greater than usual and the organisation being in frantic movement is a sign of critical moments.

28. An organisation which both exits and advances in the same field is staging a lure.

29. When the organisation lacks motivation or morale, its workforce will be deprived and latent.

30. When employees concerned over their own welfare versus the needs of the organisation, there is suffering from a lack of recognition.

31. If an organisation fails to proceed toward opportunity, then its resources are ill-prepared or exhausted.

32. When organisations gather on a given spot it is that the spot is unoccupied by a larger threat, one big move can open their eyes.

33. Being disturbed in the field shows a lack of authority. If signs of communication remain broken it will result in a lack of subordination. If the leaders are upset, it is due to a tired team.

34. An organisation willing to leave behind their direct duties for the sake of obtaining advantages shows commitment to a cause.

35. Suffering from mingling employees may be a sign of alienation, whether it is from other employees or their rank.

36. Giving extra rewards suggest the competitor is near the end of their resources. Too many punishments may show signs of strain.

37. To begin confidently unplanned to later become unsure how to remain competitive against such numbers show no sign of intelligence.

38. An organisation that receives proper invites and encouraging words from a competitor may be receiving an invite towards a cease-fire.

39. At some time, an organisation will face multitudes of competition, some making it obvious that they are in for the long haul. This requires careful evaluation and critical decision making.

40. Facing a competitor of a similar size is fine; it means there will be no direct engaging. At this point concentrate your abilities, remain watchful of your competitors, and reinforce.

41. Without the ability of forethought and knowledge of your competitors all is for sure lost.

42. Individuals not yet influenced by moral law and remain unattached to an organization will not be submissive and at that time they will hinder progress. If the individuals are influenced by moral law and punished, yet the organization does not follow through with discipline, the individuals are still considered useless and a hindrance to progress.

43. An organisation must first treat its teams with humanity but be restricted with discipline. This is the path to progress.

44. An organisation that trains its staff must be certain that commands are routinely enforced, at this point they will be well-disciplined; if this is not done, then discipline will be bad and what good then is discipline?

45. If you show confidence in your staff but always expect the teams to be obedient, there will be mutual benefits.

十 (Shí) Terrain 10

1. An organisation can compare six variations of terrain in warfare to six variations of business environments.
   (1) Accessible Ground
   (2) Entangling Ground
   (3) Temporizing Ground
   (4) Narrow Passes
   (5) Precipitous Heights
   (6) Positions at a Great Distance from the Enemy

2. Grounds accessible from all sides is accessible ground.

3. An organisation on accessible ground is facing grounds occupied by competitors. Seek precipitous heights, establish, and protect your supply to maintain an advantage.

4. Grounds easy to abort but have difficult barriers to entry is facing entangling ground.

5. An organisation on entangling grounds can overcome its competition if the competitor is unprepared. If the competition is prepared in advance and the organisation is unable to gain advantage, then to do so may become impossible, and at this point consequences will set in.

6. Temporising ground is grounds neither the organisation nor the competition gain benefit from by making the first move.

7. An organisation facing temporising grounds must not continue to progress in direct competing, even if the competitor offers bait. Pull back and remain latent. When the competition decides to progress play your move.

8. When dealing with narrow passes, be the first to occupy them and fortify them. At that point await for the preparation of your competitors.

9. If you are unable to occupy a narrow pass first then the organisation shall not attempt to occupy the pass unless lightly fortified by competition.

10. As for precipitous heights, an organisation should occupy them and remain in their chosen field to await competition to scale such heights.

11. If facing a competitor on precipitous heights don't follow them there but try and lure them away.

12. If you are a great distance from the enemy, and of equal capabilities, provoking would be difficult and competing would be to your disadvantage.

13. These six terrains are tied with earth. To carefully study them is advised to all leaders.

14. Organisations can fall victim to disasters do to the faults of their generals. If that is to happen it would need to look at these six disasters:
    (1) Flight
    (2) Insubordination
    (3) Collapse
    (4) Ruin
    (5) Disorganization
    (6) Rout

    Now comparing these disasters of warfare to business:

    (1) Flight; Downsizing, pulling back, diverting plans

    (2) Insubordination; Lack of discipline, not sticking to a plan

    (3) Collapse; Knowledge and capability issues between leaders and subordinates

    (4) Ruin; Unpermitted and haste actions taken by leaders without proper planning

(5) Disorganization; Sloppy structures, procedures, workspace, or plans limiting capability

(6) Rout; Inapropriate tactical behavior, poorly thought out strategy, poor use of resources

15. All else equal, if one object is used to engage another much larger in size the result will be the flight of the previous.

16. Insubordination spawns when employees are too experienced and their leader is too weak. Excessively strong leaders and too weak of employees leads to collapse.

17. When an organisations leaders are insubordinate you will see them taking it upon themselves to progress toward objectives not cleared through the ranks. This is ruin.

18. When leaders are weak and have no authority, when their instructions lack clarity and precision; when there are no job descriptions, when hierarchy is determined without due diligence, this is disorganization.

19. If you are unable to judge strength and to allow unmatched skillsets to progress without picking proper support or send a team to procede on something of less importance, this will end in rout.

20. These are six defeats and they should be known to all in leadership roles.

21. Terrain is an organisation's most loyal companion. An organisation needs to estimate the capabilities of the competitor, properly handle the forces leading to success, and be keen towards calculations of measurement for difficulties, dangers and discipline. Leaders must obtain and hold the skill.

22. The organisation that knows this and puts it to use will achieve more than not. Thee that doesn't nor puts it to use will surely accomplish less.

23. An organisation that knows competing will result in more than expected gains or save it from loss knows it must compete. If competing does not lead to one of these two facts, then it must not compete. A leader that goes against the organisation's wishes, and the cause leads to one of these two conclusions, then a decision must be made.

24. For an organisation to progress without the desire of recognition and fleas without shame, whose care lies in the well-being of its people and service embraces the cornerstone of organisational culture.

25. An organisation that cares for its men and women as if they are of their own blood born children will have loyal followers. This is the essence of moral law.

26. A leader that has attempted through all means and tactics to be heard, understood, obeyed, and respected for the sake of organisation, unable to smother anarchy in the ranks, must know that their children are useless, spoiled, and disobedient.

27. An organisation that knows its men are prepared to progress but is unaware that their competition is unprepared for it is not ready to succeed.

28. An organisation that knows its competitors are prepared to compete but blind to the fact their men are not is not ready to succeed.

29. An organisation that knows the competition is prepared to compete as well as its own men and women but lacks information needed to procede successfully is not ready to succeed.

30. If an organisation progresses it doesn't falter over complexity, when choosing to expand, it is never for flight.

31. If you know your organisation and you know its competitors your success is in reach. If you know heaven and earth then your success will be complete.

十一 (Shí yī) Situation 11

1. An organisation can compare the nine varieties of ground in warfare to the realm business.
   (1) Dispersive Ground
   (2) Facile Ground
   (3) Contentious Ground
   (4) Open Ground
   (5) Ground of Intersecting Highways
   (6) Serious Ground
   (7) Difficult Ground
   (8) Hemmed-In Ground
   (9) Desperate Ground

2. When an organisation is operating within its own grounds, it is called dispersive ground.

3. When an organisation has expanded into a new grounds, it is facile ground.

4. Grounds that supply great advantage to both an organization and its competitors is contentious ground.

5. Organisations that rest on the grounds that promote free movement are resting on open ground.

6. An organisation to be the first to contain subdivisions on multiple terrains, whom franchises, or partake in vertical integration are on grounds of intersecting highways and should have most under command.

7. When an organisation expands leaving behind strong competitors, it is serious ground.

8. An organisation facing complex entry barriers, difficult processes, mass legislation, many stakeholders and

shareholders, are heavy in policy, and conduct the act of business is on difficult ground.

9. When an organisation expands into niches that are unprotected risks having them exploited by another force. This is considered hemmed-in ground.

10. An organisation finding itself on desperate ground realizes that they are in a position that requires competing without delay.

11. Do not engage when on dispersive ground. Don't stop competing on facile ground. Don't compete directly on contentious ground.

12. Don't attempt prevent competition from moving on open ground. On ground of intersecting highways you must utilize allies.

13. An organisation on serious ground must forage locally or in some cases plunder, and on difficult ground keep steady progress.

14. When on hemmed-in ground resort to stratagem. When on desperate ground, compete.

15. The skilled know how to divide the competition's attention and strengths, interrupt fluency between the parts and the flanks, divide the good from the bad, and keep morale low.

16. With the competitors forces scattered, they prevented them from perfect form; even when they were united to a single objective, they managed to keep them vulnerable to disorder.

17. When it is to the organisations advantage, they progress forward; when it was not, they halted.

18. An organisation that chooses to expand or directly engage a great competitor should begin by securing

something valuable to the competitor. This way, it is the competitors loss to the organisation's gain, twice the value.

19. An initial move must be quick to take advantage of unprepared competition. An organisation must make its way by routes unknown and expand flanks to more open grounds.

20. An organisation invading grounds must take note that through expansion made deeper into competition, an organisations unity expands too and the greater the purpose will spread through the ranks. Dedication will sink in and both victories and defeats will be shared, but no competition will prevail against the organisation.

21. On new grounds with a quick incursion, an organisation should find ways to showcase products and services quickly and cost-effectively.

22. Know more than the morale of the people. Refrain from takebacks and only withhold enough dues, fees, royalties, and taxes that are needed. While concentrating on consolidation you should conserve your strength. Continuously progress and keep your men busy while providing the best calculated plans that can be delivered.

23. With assigning critical roles where success is most crucial, your men would rather achieve than fail. If facing failure and discipline there is nothing they can't achieve. Teams will put their best foot forward and work with such efficiency and effectiveness.

24. With trust in an organisation's ability to measure quantity employees facing roles lose the sense of failure. If monitored they will stay productive. If they work independently they may mingle. If there is no help they will deliver their best.

25. Without being in proper rank, employees will be in a state of preparation; They will take it upon themselves to do basic duties. Without limits they bind to moral law. They can be trusted.

26. Do not accept prognostic visions. Forbid assigning duties through religion and remove all doubts. This way until failure arises there is nothing to fear.

27. An organisation must know that employees not suffering from a lack of riches, does not mean it is because they have no interest in wealth. If an employees devoted life is short-lived, it doesn't mean they don't respect moral law.

28. There may be complaining when orders are assigned, your employees not liking the assignment, the team, or the direction of the assignment show emotions. These moments can be seen and accepted by the organisation so that all can be gained and come to rest.

29. A tactical organisation shows tactical resilience and flexibility. With these tactics, competition may have the most difficulty manipulating progress.

30. An organisation can demonstrate this tactical resilience within themselves. It can be displayed through the use of allies and even rivals with like purpose. This is simply the use of flanks and dual purpose brought about by circumstance.

31. Trust in method and discipline is not enough. Trusting your men and women to do their work without being called to arms is not enough trust.

32. The key to managing an empire is expectations. Everything has expectations. All expectations must be met through unity brought about by a single expectation devoted to all.

33. Using both the strong and weak efficiently and effectively is the answer to questions involving the use of grounds.

34. A skilled organisation leads its forces as if they are a single unit.

35. It is a leaders responsibility to uphold confidentiality; to uphold impression, to uphold method and discipline.

36. They must uphold the secrecy of information; give information on a need-to-know basis. Allow false reports, shuffling of strengths, and deceitful appearances when necessary.

37. Circumstances leading to the switching of plans and the altering of favor has perks. Uncertainties to prevail in the minds of the competitor is keeping an organisation's purpose secret.

38. Leaders act and reveal when necessary. They climb the heights with the intention of maintaining trails, guiding, leading, and shaping the realms of tomorrow as they advance into hostile grounds.

39. Organisations intend to lead. This direction or that direction is never fully known.

40. An organisation must understand that how the competition is brought into the picture is the leaders responsibility.

41. Any quantities of measurement towards and regarding the nine varieties of ground; speed of progress, the opportunities, tactics, laws of the universe must all be considered.

42. In terms of expansion, to fully compete comes consolidation and unity. To be competitive brings dispersion and divided concentration.

43. When adventuring to new grounds you will be on critical grounds. If you are in need for communication on all sides then you are on grounds of intersecting highways.

44. When fully competing you will be lead to serious ground and to be competitive means you will find yourself on facile ground.

45. With competition at your rear and narrow passes at the front you are on hemmed-in-ground and there is no time for rest on these desperate grounds.

46. You should inspire with unity on dispersive ground. On facile ground there is a need for connection between all parts of the organisation.

47. On contentious ground you need to prevent lagging and keep efficiency at your side.

48. An organisation should display more defensive tactics on open ground. Grounds of intersecting highways require alliances and consolidation.

49. On serious ground keep a steady flow of assets. An organisation that is on difficult ground must keep progressing down the chosen road.

50. While on hemmed-in-ground you are best to consider that there is no way out. While on desperate ground be honest of the situation.

51. When placed in situations employees will act with urgency. They will work hard and with stubborn resistance when they know the consequences of failure.

52. If an organisation is going to enter alliances, it must know the structure of its alliances. No man or woman is fit to lead a progressing organisation without the knowledge of both heaven and earth pertaining to their roles.

53. It is not appropriate for the occasion when an organisation isn't acknowledged for the following fundamental disciplines.

54. When an organisation expands into new markets, and its leadership prevails over the consolidation of the competition's forces. Being left mesmerized the competitors allies may be reluctant to join against you.

55. Not pressing the need to ally or to become dependent on external partnerships an organisation may maintain a chosen path yet carry out its own secrets for the sake of both personal and organisational gain.

56. Giving rewards not written in structure. Issuing orders without council. This is the way to maintain an army as if it were a single unit.

57. You should bring forth the task at hand but never the design. With the future looking positive, bring it before their eyes. Say nothing when things aren't so well.

58. To face difficulty will require an organisation to adopt different tactics but they will overcome. Choosing to prevail over falling short, they will play its role safe.

59. It is when you are threatened that you give it all you have. It is at these times an organisation may tighten down, become most efficient and achieve where it once failed.

60. Success is most accomplished when understanding the purpose of competitors.

61. Progress on the flanks of the competitor is where longterm success awaits.

62. This can be seen as organisational success through clever strategy.

63. The moment a role is accepted and objectives are clear, all future progress seizes; prior representation, strategy, and tactics stay where they are, and all is structured accordingly for new grounds.

64. Be firm in your matters so that you may control your situation.

65. If a competitor leaves an opportunity then you must take little time to consider it. If there is advantage the organisation must pursue it.

66. Stalling competition by gaining key components and capturing grounds first holds advantages. At that moment you may contemplate your competitors arrival.

67. Plan to operate by law and rules. Accept the presence of competition until you can compete on your grounds.

68. Be patient and prepared. When the competition presents an opportunity making a quick move to avoid any opposing competition would give the most favor.

十二 (Shí èr) Offense 12

1. There are ways to advance for an organisation to scorch their competition. First, is at the place of refuge. Second, is at a place of sale, Third at the supply lines and then at the place of storage. Last, is to exercise the right of dismissal. Let the five principles be known to all that attack by fire.

2. In order to implement such tactics, there must be the capability to and a reason for it. The ingredients to act with fire should not be maintained.

3. There is a proper heaven for an organisation to execute tactics of fire and days to start the process.

4. The proper heaven for an organisation to execute an attack is when times are less lucrative. The proper time to start is when it has advantage for you.

5. An organisation must be equipped to greet five potential outcomes.

6. When competition hits the place of refuge the attempt to expand externally must begin.

7. If an organisation doesn't retaliate then hold on the motion of external progress.

8. While engulfed in the competition, follow through with further progress and if that isn't possible, then hold your grounds.

9. If possible wait for a favored opportunity to progress by scorching the grounds outside and don't wait for the competition to breech the walls.

10. An organisation should remain out of the way of its actions.

11. The winds of heaven changes between day and night; stronger by day and weaker. The overall elements change between day and night; stronger by day and weaker by night or stronger by night and weaker by day.

12. The five principles should be known to every organisation, the study of the heavens should take place and proper days should be scouted.

13. The organisation that uses fire to demonstrate tactical decision shows intelligence; those who use fluid motion effectively in strength.

14. By adapting strategies of fluid motion competition can be kept at bay and not suffering full loss.

15. No organisation is fulfilled in its competing even if it leads to success without embracing the excitement and love of business. The conclusion is a bad use of time and wasted efforts while generals remain underutilized.

16. An open-minded organisation lays its plans before a scheduled date while the good leader prepares his resources.

17. An organisation shouldn't relocate or make a move unless necessary. You should only rely on others when there is something to gain. Only progress where its worth the fight.

18. An organisation doesn't lead strictly for its own cause. Nor should they progress into competition out of any form of emotion including pride.

19. If there is benefit expand; if not then stay put.

20. Moods change; mad can become glad and worries may become peace.

21. An organisation can not be brought back from ruins much like an employee can't come back to an organisation after straying too far.

22. When a leader is informed they're aware, and good leaders are cautious. This is how to remain peaceful and whole.

十三 (Shí sān) Information 13

1. The cost of maintaining operations is great. There will be loss and exhaustion on both man and the resources of the organisation. The cost will be increasingly great financially and physically. There will be times of commotion as both men and women will fall as they are dismissed from labor while on difficult trails.

2. Competition may face one another for years as they strive for dominance which is determined daily. Remaining blind to competitor positions simply for not wanting to acknowledge the expense is not the most right way for the people.

3. Organisations and people are a source of inspiration. To not be what you are meant to be may be seen as no help to the organisation and a sign of a bad leader and no subject for success.

4. It is the insight, knowledge, wisdom, and planning that allows the organisation and their great leaders to reach such great heights.

5. Knowing in advance is not brought about by the heart of a man nor by past success or failures.

6. Knowledge of the competition is gathered through other individuals.

7. There are five classes of spies that organisations know the benefits of.

   (1) Local Spies
   (2) Inward Spies
   (3) Converted Spies
   (4) Doomed Spies
   (5) Surviving Spies

8. With these spies in motion nothing may be discovered. With information an organisation is able to manipulate outcomes and that could be most sacred.

9. Local intelligence comes from local spies.

10. Inward spies come from within the competition.

11. Converted spies come from making the competition's spy one of your own.

12. Doomed spies don't plan to stay secret. They allow themselves to be known.

13. Surviving spies bring news back to the organisation.

14. Spies should be treated greatly. Relationships with spies should be maintained.

15. An organisation cannot hire a spy without the ability to understand and discriminate between their reasons and relations.

16. An organisation must be respectful and straightforward with spies.

17. An organisation must be clever enough to know they are unable to fully rely on information harnessed from their spies.

18. Spies are good in every form of business, both direct and indirect.

19. If crucial information is leaked inappropriately the relationship should end. Any leaks or threats of other individuals should be sought after and taken care of too.

20. Spies must be granted permission and empowered with proper information and granted the permissions they need to obtain what is requested.

21. Expect the use of spies and be watchful for them. Turning them into converted spies remains an option.

22. Converted spies assists in finding local spies and inward spies.

23. The converted spy assists organisations in effectively making use of doomed spies.

24. Converted spies assist an organisation with information that effectively puts the surviving spy to use on particular days.

25. The point of using spies to gather information is known to competition. This information can be obtained in an instant by a converted spy.

26. Historically, the success of empires are contributed to individuals who had both came to the likings of moral law and previously served in other, sometimes rival, group. It is their knowledge and experience that played a pivotal role in the path of long term success.

27. The enlightened organisation and its experienced well-minded leaders will use valued information from and in the use of spies to achieve results.